First Facts

OUR GOVERNMENT

SERVING ON A JURY

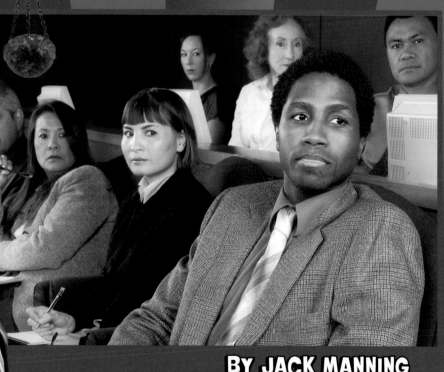

BY JACK MANNING

CAPSTONE PRESS
a capstone imprint

First Facts are published by Capstone Press,
1710 Roe Crest Drive, North Mankato, Minnesota 56003
www.capstonepub.com

Library of Congress Cataloging-in-Publication Data
Manning, Jack, author.
Serving on a jury / by Jack Manning.
    pages cm. — (First facts : our government.)
  Summary: "Informative, engaging text and vivid photos introduce readers to serving on a jury"—
Provided by publisher.
  Includes bibliographical references and index.
  ISBN 978-1-4914-0333-4 (library binding)
  ISBN 978-1-4914-0337-2 (paperback)
  ISBN 978-1-4914-0341-9 (eBook PDF)
1. Jury—United States—Juvenile literature. I. Title.
  KF8972.M25 2015
  347.73′52—dc23   2014004759

Editorial Credits
Brenda Haugen, editor; Heidi Thompson, designer; Eric Gohl, media researcher;
Katy LaVigne, production specialist

Photo Credits
Getty Images: The Image Bank/David Young-Wolff, 5, 17, The Image Bank/Ron Chapple, 21, Image
Source, 13; iStockphotos: Alina555, 1 (right), Moodboard_Images, cover, Rich Legg, 11; Newscom:
EPA/POOL/Doug Pizac, 9, EPA/POOL/Robert Gauthier, 19; Shutterstock: bikeriderlondon, 7, 15,
Evok20, cover (background), Jorg Hackemann, cover (statue), 1 (left)

Printed in China by Nordica
0414/CA21400593
032014   008095NORDF14

TABLE OF CONTENTS

CHAPTER 1

COURT CASES

Have you ever had a hard time making a decision about a rule? Sometimes people can't make decisions about laws themselves. When people need help, they go to courts. Courts are part of the U.S. government's **judicial branch**.

Courts make decisions based on the **Constitution**. The Constitution gives people the right to a jury **trial**. A jury is a group of people who listens to the facts during a trial. They decide who is right.

judicial branch—the part of the government that explains laws
Constitution—the written system of laws in the United States; it states the rights of the people and the powers of government
trial—the court process to decide if a charge or claim is true

CHAPTER 2

JURY MEMBERS

Jury members are chosen from the communities where the trials will be held. In the United States, most juries have 12 members called jurors. Some juries have six members.

Not everyone can serve on a jury. In most states people must be at least 18 years old to be on a jury. They need to be U.S. **citizens** and speak English.

citizen—a member of a country, state, or city who has the right to live there

FACT Jurors are often chosen from lists of voters or from those with drivers licenses.

CHAPTER 3

DECIDING CASES

Have you ever heard the saying there are two sides to every story? That is true of court **cases** too. All cases have two sides. In a trial the government or a **plaintiff** can bring a case against a **defendant**.

Juries decide cases about people, property, and laws. Some trials solve problems between people. In other trials juries decide if someone broke a law.

case—a suit or action in law
plaintiff—someone who brings a legal case against a defendant
defendant—the person in a court case who may have broken a law or caused a legal problem

CHAPTER 4

LAWYERS HELP PEOPLE

In court **lawyers** ask **witnesses** to give facts about the case. Some lawyers help the defendant. Other lawyers work for the plaintiff.

lawyers—a person who is trained to advise people about the law

witness—a person who has seen or heard something

A lawyer asks a witness questions.

Lawyers for each side state facts and show **evidence** in court. Outside of court they study laws. They also question people who know about the case. All of these things help prove their cases.

 **FACT** Most trials last less than one week. The longest trial lasted more than 2½ years.

evidence—information, items, and facts that help prove something is true or false

CHAPTER 5

JUDGES LEAD THE COURTS

Judges are in charge of courts. They answer questions about laws. Judges tell juries about laws and decide if evidence is **illegal**. Judges make sure everyone follows the rules in court.

illegal—against the law

FACT Many judges went from town to town on horses to hear cases in the 1700s and 1800s.

CHAPTER 6

FOLLOWING RULES

Juries must follow court rules. A jury listens to both sides of a case. Jury members can't talk about the case with other people. Jurors can't read or listen to news about the case. These rules help juries make fair decisions.

FACT In the United States, about 5 million people are called for jury service each year.

A jury gathers to reach a decision on a case.

CHAPTER 7

MAKING VERDICTS

After lawyers present their cases, jurors meet in private. Jurors talk about the evidence of the case. Then jury members vote on a **verdict**.

Verdicts decide jury cases. A juror reads the verdict in court. The judge explains the jury's decision and gives a **sentence** or punishment.

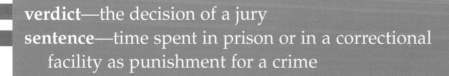

verdict—the decision of a jury
sentence—time spent in prison or in a correctional facility as punishment for a crime

CHAPTER 8

PROTECTING RIGHTS

Serving on a jury is every citizen's duty. In the United States, juries protect a person's right to a fair trial. Juries make sure that people are treated fairly in court.

Amazing but True!

How long can you go without using your computer or watching TV? What about calling your friends or family on the phone? Sometimes jurors are not allowed to do these things. In fact they might not even be allowed to go home during a trial. A judge can order jurors to stay overnight in a hotel until a case is decided. Jurors stay in a hotel to make sure they do not hear or read news about a case. Jurors can stay in hotels for a few days or many weeks. While there jurors can't use computers, watch TV, or read newspapers. They also can't use telephones.

GLOSSARY

case (KAYSS)—a legal problem settled in court

citizen (SIT-i-zuhn)—a member of a country, state, or city who has the right to live there

Constitution (con-stuh-TOO-shuhn)—the written system of laws in the United States; it states the rights of the people and the powers of government

defendant (di-FEN-duhnt)—the person in a court case who may have broken a law or caused a legal problem

evidence (E-vuh-duhnss)—information, items, and facts that help prove something is true or false

illegal (i-LEE-guhl)—against the law

judicial branch (joo-DISH-uhl BRANCH)—the part of government that explains laws

lawyer (LAW-yur)—a person who is trained to advise people about the law

plaintiff (PLAYN-tif)—someone who brings a legal case against a defendant

sentence (SEN-tuhnss)—time spent in prison or a correctional facility as punishment for a crime

trial (TRYE-uhl)—the court process to decide if a charge or claim is true

verdict (VUR-dikt)—the decision of a jury

witness (WIT-niss)—a person who has seen or heard something

READ MORE

DiPrimio, Pete. *The Judicial Branch*. My Guide to the Constitution. Hockessin, Del.: M. Lane, 2012.

Harris, Nancy. *What's the State Judicial Branch?* First Guide to Government. Chicago: Heinemann Library, 2008.

Kowalski, Kathiann M. *Judges and Courts: A Look at the Judicial Branch*. How Does Government Work? Minneapolis: Lerner Publications, 2012.

INTERNET SITES

FactHound offers a safe, fun way to find Internet sites related to this book. All of the sites on FactHound have been researched by our staff.

Here's all you do:

Visit *www.facthound.com*

Type in this code: 9781491403334

Check out projects, games and lots more at
www.capstonekids.com

INDEX

CRITICAL THINKING USING THE COMMON CORE

1. Juries make sure that people get fair trials. How do they do this? (Key Ideas and Details)
2. Can you remember a time when you believe you were treated unfairly? What evidence can you present to make your case? Would you win your case? (Integration of Knowledge and Ideas)